Power Up!

Story by Michael Pryor

Illustrations by Scott Brown

Power Up!

Text: Michael Pryor
Publishers: Tania Mazzeo and Eliza Webb
Series consultant: Amanda Sutera
Hands on Heads Consulting
Editor: Sarah Layton
Project editor: Annabel Smith
Designer: Jess Kelly
Project designer: Danielle Maccarone
Illustrations: Scott Brown
Production controller: Renee Tome

NovaStar

ISBN 978 0 17 033474 7

Cengage Learning Australia
Level 5, 80 Dorcas Street
Southbank VIC 3006 Australia
Phone: 1300 790 853
Email: aust.nelsonprimary@cengage.com

For learning solutions, visit **cengage.com.au**

Printed in China by 1010 Printing International Ltd
1 2 3 4 5 6 7 29 28 27 26 25

Nelson acknowledges the Traditional Owners and Custodians of the lands of all First Nations Peoples. We pay respect to Elders past and present, and extend that respect to all First Nations Peoples today.

Contents

CLEAN
ENERGY

Chapter 1

Project Problems

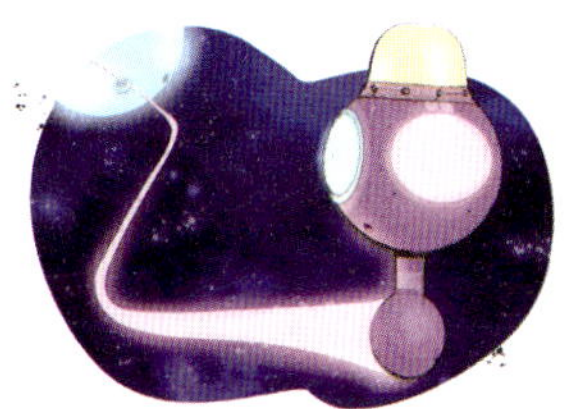

Archer and Liam were working on their school science project in Archer's garage. They were nearly done, but the finishing touches were proving tricky.

"Remember," Liam said, "when we finish this project, we're going to be the total and absolute experts in everything to do with clean energy!"

Archer rolled his eyes. "You keep saying that, but I don't see you doing much to help us."

"I am!" Liam said. "So much researching, so many websites, so much reading ..."

"You've only read half as much as me," Archer interrupted.

Liam grinned. "That's why we're a good team! You're the brains, and I bring a can-do attitude. Now, hold that panel steady while I screw it in, or we'll never win first prize."

"I *am* holding it steady," Archer said.

Their project stretched across the table, a model solar farm with twelve tiny solar panels. Each panel was the size of a playing card and made of layers of glass and silicon wafers. They were very delicate, but the solar panels would generate enough electricity to light up an impressive "Clean Energy" sign.

Archer thought their model was a total winner. "Hurry up with the screwdriver," he told Liam.

"I'd be quicker if you moved your hand out of the way," Liam replied.

"If I move my hand, everything's going to fall over," Archer warned.

"Look, don't distract me," Liam said.

"I'm getting a cramp in my thumb," Archer warned again. "Hurry up."

"Done." Liam took a step back, grinning. Then he tripped on a bike helmet Archer had left on the floor. "Waargh!"

Archer tried to catch Liam as he fell, but Liam's elbow swiped one of the solar panels. Archer watched open-mouthed as the first panel toppled. It fell against the one next to it. Then, the carefully arranged panels fell over one by one, like a row of dominoes. Glass cracked and shattered.

CLEAN ENERGY

Archer groaned at the disaster zone. “It took us two weeks to get this far,” he said. “We’ll never get it finished in time!”

“And we’ve got to hand it in tomorrow,” Liam pointed out.

But Archer hardly heard him because from outside came a loud crackling noise, followed by a boom of something like thunder with a weird, low humming edge. The garage roof shook. Both boys stared at the sudden cloud of dust that floated down from the rafters.

A knock came at the garage door. Archer opened it, and he and Liam stared.

A strange creature stood there, looking like a giant, bright-blue lizard.

Chapter 2

The Spaceship

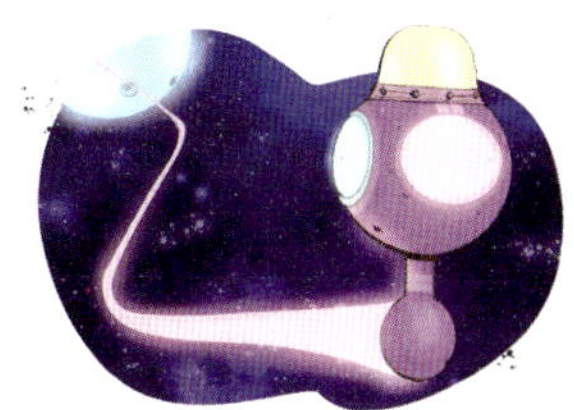

The creature waved a three-fingered, webbed hand. "Hello! I am Bodman! I am from the planet Gandoody! My monitoring device has told me that you are the total and absolute experts in everything to do with clean energy? Good! I need your help!"

The boys stood there, stunned.

Bodman went on. "I have to do a school project on how creatures on other planets have found new ways to generate clean energy." He stepped into the garage while Archer and Liam stared. "It must be handed in very soon, but my work partner is extremely lazy and has done no work."

Archer couldn't believe it. An alien was talking to him!

"I know how you feel," Liam said. "I have to do all the work on our project because my partner hasn't got a clue."

"As if!" Archer said to Liam. He turned back to Bodman. "I have to do all the work because *my* partner keeps breaking things."

"Truly?" Bodman asked, flapping his webbed hands in the air. "That is terrible! You should both run away from your work partners with much speed!"

"It's okay, we're joking." Archer nudged Liam. "Just kidding around."

"I was warned about Earth humour. It is difficult to understand." Bodman flapped his hands again. "If you cannot help me, I will have to find some other experts to tour this planet in my spaceship and study clean energy."

Archer looked at Liam. "Am I dreaming?"

"Are we talking to a blue alien?" Liam asked.

"Yes," Archer replied.

"Then we're not dreaming," Liam said.

"And did he just invite us to go with him on his spaceship?" Archer asked.

"He did! Sounds like a great opportunity."

Archer grinned. "I've been dying for a trip in a spaceship."

Bodman flapped his hands again. "You will not die! I am a very careful pilot!"

Archer groaned. It looked like they'd need to help Bodman understand how people say things on Earth.

Chapter 3

Waves

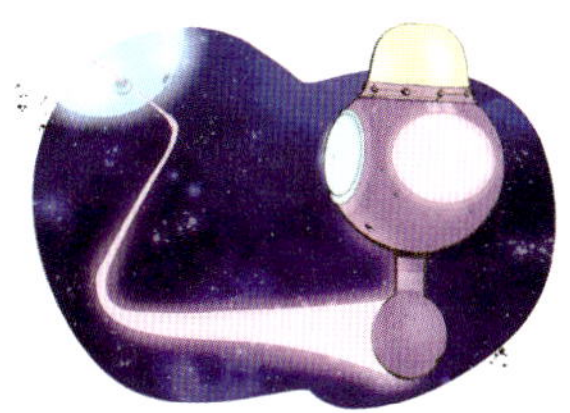

While Bodman poked around the garage, looking in amazement at an old lawn mower, Liam and Archer put their heads together for a quick discussion.

"We've learnt a lot for our project, so I'm sure we can help Bodman with his," Archer said.

"Of course we can!" Liam said. "After all, we are the total and absolute experts in everything to do with clean energy, remember?"

"Maybe we haven't hit expert level *just* yet," Archer pointed out.

"Come on! We've been emailing energy researchers and asking authorities – and our teacher has been a big help, too," Liam said. "We can do this!"

"All right," Archer said, and they high-fived.

Quickly, they talked about the types of power and different energy-generating facilities they had investigated.

"Can you take us to Hawaii?" Archer asked Bodman, finally. "There's a power plant in the ocean there that makes electricity using the movement of waves."

"Excellent! Come this way." Bodman marched out of the garage. A spaceship was in Archer's backyard, right next to the plum tree. It was smaller than Archer expected, not much bigger than an ordinary car. It sat on three legs, was round and had a large, clear bubble on top.

"That's the best spaceship I've seen all day," Liam said.

They followed Bodman and piled in. Archer found a seat, but he was almost too excited to sit still. It was a real, proper spaceship!

"Now," Bodman said. "Show me Hawaii on my map."

Bodman pointed to a screen near the steering column of the spaceship. Liam studied it and pointed at Hawaii.

"It will take us fourteen snorgsnaps to get there," Bodman said. "That is about half of one of your Earth hours."

"Whoa," Archer said. "That's fast!"

Then, Archer felt something wet on the back of his neck. He turned to find a furry creature licking him with a long, bright-green tongue. "Waargh!" cried Archer.

Liam, sitting next to Archer, squawked, "Help!"

Bodman made a chuffing noise. The creature leapt over Archer and Liam into Bodman's arms. "Do not be afraid!" Bodman said. "This is my pet snorker, Feggibell."

The snorker was about the size and shape of a watermelon. It had four legs, brown straggly fur and a tail like a bunch of rags tied together.

Liam leaned over to Archer. "That's the weirdest pet I've ever seen," he murmured.

Archer nodded. The snorker had one green eye and the other was purple. It licked Bodman's face – and its tongue smelt very much like oranges.

"Feggibell and I go everywhere together," Bodman said. "You can hold her if you wish."

Archer ended up with the alien pet on his lap while they streaked across the sky in the spaceship. Liam reached over and patted Feggibell very carefully, and soon she was making a rumbling, grunting sound that Archer guessed was her way of purring.

Below the spaceship, land hurtled by and clouds rushed past outside the clear bubble. Soon, they were zooming over the ocean. In no time at all, they arrived at a bay off the coast of Hawaii, and Bodman had them circling over the wave power plant. Two big, upright yellow cylinders floated on the surface of the water.

"How does it work?" Bodman asked.

Archer had the facts ready. “The yellow cylinders move up and down in the waves and drive the shafts that generate the electricity.”

“Big cables connect the power plant to the seabed and hold it in place,” Liam added. “You don’t want your wave-power generator drifting all over the bay.”

“Astounding!” Bodman said.

They circled above the power plant so Bodman could take photos. After a while, Liam yawned. "Hey, Bodman. Time for a break."

Bodman flapped his hands. "I do not want to break anything! I have much work to do!"

"Liam means that we should have a rest," Archer said. "How about landing under that coconut tree so we can stretch our legs?"

"You want your legs to be longer?" Bodman asked. But he landed the spaceship on an out-of-the-way beach.

They climbed out onto the hot sand. Archer wiped his forehead. Just offshore, the big yellow cylinders bobbed slowly.

While Liam, Bodman and Feggibell splashed in the shallows, Archer frowned. Was that another spaceship in the distance? He turned to ask Bodman, but just then, Feggibell launched herself out of the water. She knocked Archer down and sat on his chest, snuffling happily in his face.

"I think she likes you," Liam said to Archer.

Chapter 4

Dazzled

Archer and Liam agreed that a solar farm would be their next destination.

Liam used the navigation screen. "There! Northern Australia. A huge solar farm."

Bodman was puzzled. "You farm the sun?"

"We make electricity from sunshine," Archer said. "Australia is a very sunny continent, so we can generate lots of clean energy efficiently there."

"Remarkable," Bodman said, and soon they were circling the solar farm.

"There are more than a million solar panels down there," Liam said.

"And this farm can make enough electricity to power more than 200 000 homes," Archer added.

"That is very good-quality information," Bodman said. "I am sure my science project will be the best!"

Archer was looking down at the solar panels and thought he saw some movement. Was it a kangaroo or a person, he wondered? Or something else?

Suddenly, the spaceship was filled with dazzling light. Archer put his hands over his eyes. Liam yelled and Feggibell squealed. The spaceship started spinning wildly, and Archer was thrown from side to side.

"I cannot see!" Bodman wailed. "Automatic pilot, please take over!"

The spinning slowed and came to a stop. Archer took his hands from his eyes. Spots and colours danced in his vision, but they soon began to clear.

"What happened?" Liam asked as he rubbed his eyes.

"The sunshine reflected off a solar panel and dazzled us," Bodman said.

"I thought I saw something down there, moving the panels," Archer said. "Or someone."

Bodman flapped his hands. "No, no, it was an accident. Nothing strange is happening."

But Archer wasn't so sure.

Chapter 5

Yellow Cloud

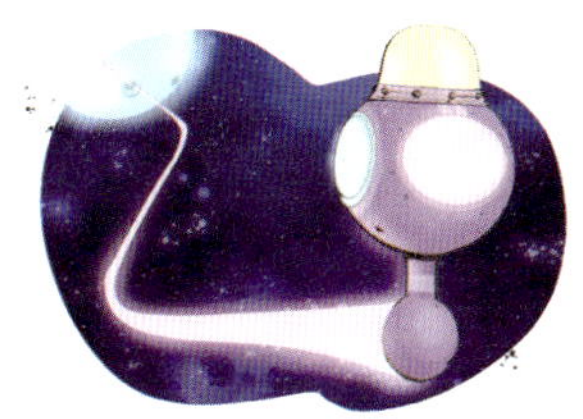

"Next, a geothermal plant!" Liam exclaimed.

"What is a geothermal plant?" Bodman asked.

"A geothermal plant uses heat from deep in the earth to make steam," Archer explained. "The steam then generates electricity."

Liam moved Feggibell aside so he could reach the navigation screen. She snorted happily when he scratched her ear.

"She really likes you," Archer said to Liam.

"There," Liam said, pointing at the navigation screen. "New Zealand. It has active volcanoes, which makes it the perfect place to build a geothermal plant."

"Energy from volcanoes!" said Bodman, waving his hands. "How exciting."

About nine snorgsnaps later, when they came close, Liam pointed. "See all the steam? That's New Zealand's biggest geothermal power plant. It can make enough electricity to power 160 000 homes!"

"Incredible!" Bodman said. "There is nothing like this on Gandoody. I will take pictures!"

They hovered over the pipes, towers, buildings and swirling clouds of steam. Feggibell gave a rumbly bark. Bodman reached around and patted her. "Feggibell has a sensitive nose. She does not like the smell."

Archer shrugged. "Those yellowish clouds are sulfur. A bit stinky, but mostly harmless."

"We're working on all sorts of other ways to generate clean electricity," Liam said. "Wind power, hydropower – we've got lots to show you."

But Bodman wasn't listening. His mouth was open, and he was staring into the distance. Archer looked in the same direction. Was that another spaceship out there?

"What's wrong, Bodman?" Liam asked.

"Hold on, please," Bodman said. "Very tightly."

Bodman's spaceship tilted, then tipped and dived. Archer hung onto his seat while Liam whooped. "All right!" he cried. "Aerobatics!"

Feggibell squealed as the spaceship made a hard right turn, then pulled into a fast spiral. Archer was dizzy as Bodman sent the ship into a steep climb. Outside, sulfur clouds whipped up behind them and flew towards whatever it was Archer had seen in the sky.

Archer shook his head, mostly to see if it was still attached. “What was all that about?”

“Nothing,” Bodman said. “Nothing at all,” he repeated as he settled the spaceship into its usual, calm flight.

Archer and Liam looked at each other. Something strange was going on, that was certain.

Chapter 6

A Confession

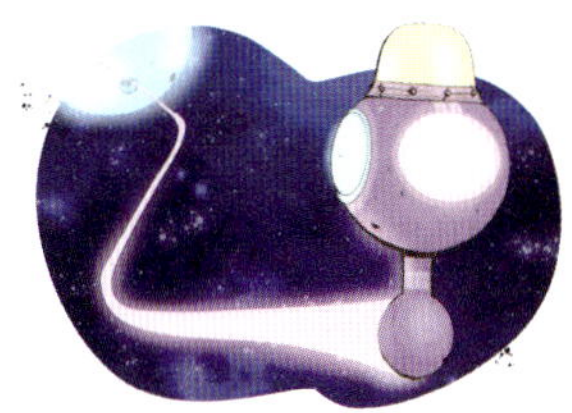

"Come on, Bodman," Liam said. "What was that swooping and diving for?"

Bodman's shoulders sagged. Feggibell nudged him, but he took no notice. "Let us land and stretch our arms," he said. "I have a confession."

Bodman found an isolated hill and landed the spaceship in a clearing. Everyone got out and Bodman sighed. "My worst enemy is here."

Archer and Liam shared a look. What had they let themselves in for?

"Argaz was my school project partner," Bodman went on. "The one who is extremely lazy and has done no work. He has a spaceship, too, and he has been following us. He is so lazy, and he will not do any work of his own. Instead, he wants to steal mine."

“Sounds like a true enemy,” Liam said.

“It is worse than that,” Bodman continued. “Argaz was my friend. The best project wins a magnificent prize, but Argaz wants it all for himself.”

“What sort of prize?” Liam asked.

“The winner receives much money and a first-class tour of the galaxy and gets to star in a major action movie.”

Archer blinked. “That’s a lot better than the first prize for our project.”

“What is your prize?” Bodman asked.

“A free trip to the Galaxy World Amusement Park,” Archer said.

“With a gold pass for free rides all day,” Liam said. “We’ve researched it carefully so we can maximise our time there. We’re going to ride the giant drop, then we’re going to stay on the Ferris wheel for hours.”

“A world that is a galaxy?” Bodman asked. “A galaxy that is a world? This makes no sense!”

“An amusement park is a place where people go to scare themselves silly to have fun,” Archer explained with a smile.

Bodman sighed. “I will never understand Earth people.”

Archer shook his head. "I don't understand Argaz. He's travelled across the galaxy to steal your work? That's more effort than doing the project himself!"

"I do very excellent work," Bodman said. "And he is very lazy."

"We'll just have to make sure he doesn't follow us to our next destination," Liam said.

"I am trying," Bodman said. "At the geothermal plant, I hurled the sulfur cloud at him to drive him away after he dazzled us by tilting the panels at the solar farm."

"Never mind," Liam said. "We'll help you collect some up-to-date information that he doesn't have. That way, you'll have a winning science project, for sure."

Bodman snuffled a little. "You are very kind, Earth friends."

Archer rubbed his chin thoughtfully. "Whenever we find a good electricity-generation plant, Argaz follows us right there."

Bodman's eyes widened. "Argaz must have used a tracking device! Wait here!"

When he came back from the spaceship, Bodman was upset. “I have found a tracking device behind your seat. Argaz has been able to follow us, and he has been listening to us, too. He has all the excellent information you have been sharing with me!”

“Let’s get the device and throw it away!” Liam said. “Let him try to follow us then!”

Archer grabbed Bodman’s arm. “Wait! I think we can use this tracking device to make sure Argaz fails at his cheating while Bodman finishes a sensational project.”

“Of course we can,” Liam said, scratching his head. “How, exactly?”

Archer grinned. “How good are you at acting, Bodman?”

Chapter 7

The Giant Wheel

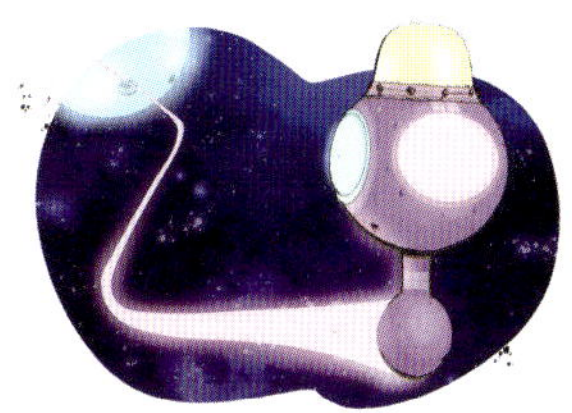

Archer, Liam and Bodman sat under a clump of shady trees to discuss Archer's plan. "If we talk about a clean-energy-generating plant that's actually completely fake," Archer suggested, "Argaz will overhear and include it in his project. It'll be a disaster for him!"

"He is so lazy that he will do just that," Bodman said. "Perfect!"

Feggibell ran around in circles, chasing her tail and snorting happily.

After Archer, Liam and Bodman rehearsed how they would discuss a fake clean-energy-generating plant so Argaz would hear about it through the tracking device, they took off. While they were travelling, Archer and Liam started acting.

"The giant wheel is the most modern, most amazing clean-energy-generating machine anywhere," Liam said.

"It's huge," Archer said. "A spectacular sight, and a fantastic new way to generate clean energy."

Liam went on to tell Bodman that the giant wheel was a hundred metres tall. Archer explained how it was a tourist attraction as well as a source of power. They even talked about how it was constructed and what the tickets cost.

Bodman played his part. He said things like "Tell me more" and "Extra details, please".

Archer found it hard to stop grinning. All their planning for a trip to the Galaxy World Amusement Park was proving to be valuable!

Soon, they were flying over the amusement park. It was full of people, and all the rides were packed with happy customers. Archer nudged Bodman and pointed. While Liam grinned, Bodman brought the spaceship around so that it circled Galaxy World's big Ferris wheel.

"And there's the giant wheel," Archer said. "The newest, most revolutionary clean power invention on Earth."

"The giant wheel is going to transform the world," Liam said. "And people are going to have fun at the same time."

"It's rotating!" Bodman said. "With people inside!"

"Wheels have been part of making power ever since the olden days," Archer said. "The wheel going around drives the generators and creates electricity."

"The incredible thing here is that the giant wheel uses passengers to make it go around and around," Liam said. "When the weight of the passengers on one side isn't the same as the other, then the wheel is unbalanced, and it turns."

Archer had trouble keeping a straight face. This was all nonsense, of course! But he continued. "It's very complicated, so it's done with computers to make sure that the wheel is uneven in just the right way. Once it starts turning, people have to swap places to keep it going, but that's part of the fun."

"And people actually pay to go on it!" Liam said. "The giant wheel generates power and makes money, while the people on it pay for the fun experience!"

Archer was impressed by Liam's acting. He hoped Argaz was listening to every word.

"And you say this is very new?" Bodman said. "Excellent! My project will have the most up-to-date information! I'm sure to win first prize!"

"Good luck to you," Archer said.

"I think I have enough information now," Bodman said. "Thank you, Earth friends. I will take you home."

Chapter 8

Home Time

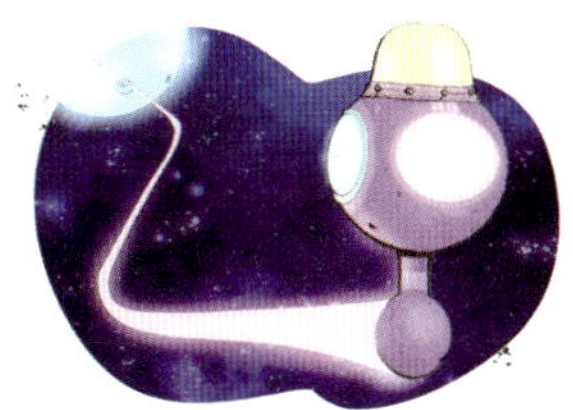

When they arrived back at Archer's place, Bodman insisted on helping Archer and Liam restore their broken project. "You helped me so much, I want to help you."

With three pairs of hands, the model solar farm was quickly fixed and finished. A few alien tweaks even made the "Clean Energy" sign change colours in dazzling patterns.

Feggibell helped by waddling around the table and rubbing up against people's legs.

Finally, after admiring the finished project, Bodman said it was time to leave. "But before I go, I have a gift for you both."

He handed them each a small globe. Inside each globe was a lifelike hologram of Feggibell.

"You both like Feggibell so much," he said, "these can remind you of her when we have gone."

Liam leaned down and scratched Feggibell behind the ear. "You're a gorgeous snorker, aren't you?"

Bodman and Feggibell climbed into the spaceship. Bodman waved both hands as they took off.

Archer studied the Feggibell globe. "I'm pretty sure no one else has one of these," he said.

Liam shook his. "How cool! We have alien holo-globes!"

Archer and Liam's science project won second prize, which they both thought was pretty good, even if they didn't get to go to Galaxy World.

The next day, they were in Archer's garage cleaning up when they received a message from Bodman.

Argaz had presented his project and had made it entirely about the giant wheel. The teacher had asked him to do it again – with no jokes this time. Defeated, he had approached Bodman and apologised for stealing his research and making his work difficult. Bodman told him the truth about the giant wheel, then he helped Argaz do his project properly, and they were friends again.

Attached to the message was a holo-photo of Bodman and Argaz with a happy-looking Feggibell.

"That sure was an amazing adventure," Archer said to Liam.

"And now we're *definitely* the total and absolute experts in clean energy," Liam said. "Aren't we?"

"Close enough," Archer said, grinning. "Close enough."